This
Book
Belongs
To _

Grolier Enterprises Inc.
SHERMAN TURNPIKE, DANBURY, CONNECTICUT 06816

Book Club Edition

The STORY Of PAUL

Written by Alice Joyce Davidson
Designed by Victoria Marshall

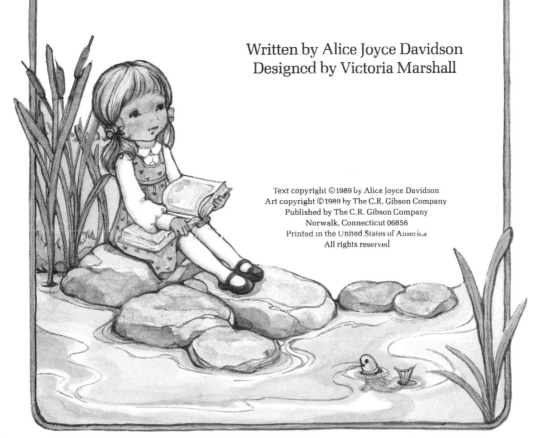

Text copyright ©1989 by Alice Joyce Davidson
Art copyright ©1989 by The C.R. Gibson Company
Published by The C.R. Gibson Company
Norwalk, Connecticut 06856
Printed in the United States of America

A girl whose name was Alice
Sat on a comfy stool
Studying some lessons
For her class in Bible school.

She chose a thrilling story
About a man named Saul,
And how he was converted
To become a man named Paul.

As Alice read she heard a knock,
And on her windowsill
The airmail bird was waiting
With this letter in his bill:

"Reading is the magic key
To take you where you want to be."

The storybook that Alice read
Became a giant screen.
Alice walked on through to Bibleland
And came upon this scene.

She saw a man whose name was Saul,
And much to her surprise,
The story she was reading
Came to life before her eyes.

Saul was mean and horrid,
He was nasty through and through.
He liked to hunt for Christians,
Then persecute them, too.

He was traveling to Damascus,
Where he was sure there'd be
More Christians he could lock in jail,
Then throw away the key.

Suddenly a bright white light
Was shining all around.
The light had come from heaven,
And Saul fell to the ground.

Out of nowhere came a voice
That made this solemn plea,
"Saul, please tell me why you are
Persecuting me?"

"Who are you?" Saul asked trembling,
As the voice came from the sky.
"I'm Jesus whom you're persecuting,"
Came the quick reply.

Surprised and quite astonished,
And shaking through and through,
Saul said, "Lord, please tell me
What would you have me do?"

"Get up and travel onward
To Damascus just ahead.
There you'll find out what to do,"
The voice of Jesus said.

Now, the men who were with Saul
Were all speechless as can be,
For they, too, heard a voice cry out,
From no one they could see.

The bright light left Saul blind, and so
The others led the way.
They took him to Damascus
Where he could rest and pray.

For three long lonely days, still blind,
Saul didn't eat a bite.
Instead, he prayed and prayed and prayed,
All through each day and night.

Later on, a holy man
Who followed Jesus' ways,
Had a vision of the Lord
Who said, "Go where Saul stays."

Ananais had heard of Saul,
How nasty he had been,
And didn't want to go to Saul
Or help him see again.

But the Lord insisted that he go.
He'd chosen Saul to spread
The news of His forgiveness
In the days that lay ahead.

Ananais went to Saul and said,
"The Lord has sent me by."
Then gently laid his healing hands,
One upon each eye.

Saul was truly thankful
That he could see again.
He asked Jesus to forgive him
And he was baptized there and then.

He changed his name from Saul to Paul.
And on that very day,
He became a Christian
And followed Jesus' way.

Then Paul began to travel
And he told everyone
The Good News that Jesus loves us,
And Jesus is God's Son.

And all who heard Paul's preaching
Were amazed as they could be,
For Paul, who once jailed Christians,
Now spread Christianity.

Paul traveled over land and sea,
And he wrote letters, too,
That taught about God's gift of love,
As he was meant to do.

The time had come for Alice
To leave that Bible scene.
She went back home by walking through
Her storybook's big screen.

Alice put her book away.
She sat down on her stool,
And thought, "I've learned a lot to share
With friends at Bible school.

"When Ananais obeyed God and
Helped restore Paul's sight,
Paul accepted Jesus
And he truly saw the light.

"And after his baptism,
Paul not only changed his name,
He changed his way of living,
He never was the same.

"Paul sought out unbelievers
And preached to everyone
The Good News that God loves us
And Jesus is God's Son.

"Paul was able to help others,
And free them of their sin,
As they accepted Jesus
And let His spirit in.

"And just like Paul, who started out
With mean and nasty ways,
We, too, can change and fill our hearts
With Jesus through our days!"